Differentiated Reading
for Comprehension

Grade 2

Credits
Content Editor: Shirley Pearson
Copy Editor: Karen Seberg
Illustrations: Nick Greenwood, Donald O'Connor

 Visit *carsondellosa.com* for correlations to Common Core, state, national, and Canadian provincial standards.

Carson-Dellosa Publishing, LLC
PO Box 35665
Greensboro, NC 27425 USA
carsondellosa.com

Printed in the USA • All rights reserved.   ISBN 978-1-4838-0487-3

01-034141151

Table of Contents

Introduction

Providing all students access to high quality, nonfiction text is essential to Common Core State Standards mastery. This book contains exactly what teachers are looking for: high-interest nonfiction passages, each written at three different reading levels, followed by a shared set of text-dependent comprehension questions and a writing prompt to build content knowledge. Both general academic and domain-specific vocabulary words are reinforced at the end of each passage for further comprehension support. The standards listed on each page provide an easy reference tool for lesson planning, and the Common Core Alignment Chart on page 3 allows you to target or remediate specific skills.

The book is comprised of 15 stories that are written at three levels:
- Below level (one dot beside the page number): 1 to 1.5 levels below grade level
- On level (two dots beside the page number): 0 to 0.5 levels below grade level
- Advanced (three dots beside the page number): 1 to 2 levels above grade level

Which students will not enjoy reading about a mouse-sized monkey or the ghost of a president or a long ride just for doughnuts? This book will quickly become the go-to resource for differentiated nonfiction reading practice in your classroom!

Common Core Alignment Chart

Common Core State Standards*		Practice Pages
Reading Standards for Informational Text		
Key Ideas and Details	2.RI.1–2.RI.3	7, 11, 15, 19, 23, 27, 31, 35, 39, 43, 47, 51, 55, 59, 63
Craft and Structure	2.RI.4–2.RI.6	4–6, 8–10, 12–14, 15, 16–18, 20–22, 24–26, 28–30, 32–34, 36–38, 39, 40–42, 44–46, 48–50, 52–54, 56–58, 59, 60–62, 63
Integration of Knowledge and Ideas	2.RI.7–2.RI.9	7, 11, 23, 39, 63
Range of Reading and Level of Text Complexity	2.RI.10	4–6, 8–10, 12–14, 16–18, 20–22, 24–26, 28–30, 32–34, 36–38, 40–42, 44–46, 48–50, 52–54, 56–58, 60–62
Reading Standards: Foundational Skills		
Phonics and Word Recognition	2.RF.3	47
Fluency	2.RF.4	4–6, 8–10, 12–14, 16–18, 20–22, 24–26, 28–30, 32–34, 36–38, 40–42, 44–46, 47, 48–50, 52–54, 55, 56–58, 60–62
Writing Standards		
Text Types and Purposes	2.W.1–2.W.3	7, 11, 15, 23, 27, 31, 35, 39, 43, 47, 51, 55, 59, 63
Production and Distribution of Writing	2.W.5–2.W.6	7, 15, 19, 31, 35
Language Standards		
Conventions of Standard English	2.L.1–2.L.2	19, 23, 27, 31, 35, 39, 43, 51
Knowledge of Language	2.L.3	11, 15, 23, 43, 55, 59
Vocabulary Acquisition and Use	2.L.4–2.L.6	4–6, 7, 8–10, 11, 12–14, 16–18, 19, 20–22, 24–26, 27, 28–30, 31, 32–34, 35, 36–38, 40–42, 43, 44–46, 47, 48–50, 51, 52–54, 55, 56–58, 59, 60–62, 63

* © Copyright 2010. National Governors Association Center for Best Practices and Council of Chief State School Officers. All rights reserved.

How to Use This Alignment Chart

The Common Core State Standards for English Language Arts are a shared set of expectations for each grade level in the areas of reading, writing, speaking, listening, and language. They define what students should understand and be able to do. This chart presents the standards that are covered in this book.

Use this chart to plan your instruction, practice, or remediation of a specific standard. To do this, first choose your targeted standard; then, find the pages listed on the chart that correlate to the standard you are teaching. Finally, assign the reading pages and follow-up questions to practice the skill.

Biggest Bill on the Block

Have you ever seen a toucan? It is a hard bird to miss! Its **bill** is huge! It is colorful too. A toucan's bill is yellow, orange, and black. Some toucans also have green and red in their bills. With a bill that big, might the toucan fall over? It does not fall over because the bill is very light.

A toucan's bill has jagged edges. These edges are like teeth. This lets the toucan eat different foods. Toucans eat fruit and tree frogs. They even eat other birds' eggs!

Why is the toucan's bill so big? Maybe it scares away **enemies**. Maybe it helps the bird get food from long tree branches. Maybe it has no special use at all. Scientists cannot agree!

The toucan has strange feet. It has four toes. Two toes face forward. Two toes face backward. Toucans live in the rain forest. Their toes help them stand on wet branches.

The toucan has a strange tongue too. The tongue has bristles on its end. These are like sharp hairs. The bristles help the bird make a croaking sound. Toucans are very loud. You can hear a toucan from far away!

Toucans do not live alone. They live in groups. Six or more toucans live in one **flock**. Toucans live in **hollow** trees. This is where they make their nests. They sleep together inside the tree. Both parents sit on the eggs. Both parents feed the chicks.

Toucans are strange looking. But, they are friendly. This makes them easy to tame when they live in a zoo.

bill: a bird's mouth, also called a beak
enemy: someone or something harmful or destructive
flock: a group of animals or people
hollow: empty inside

2.RI.4, 2.RI.10, 2.RF.4, 2.L.4

Biggest Bill on the Block

Have you ever seen a toucan? It is a hard bird to miss! It has a huge yellow, orange, and black **bill**. Some toucans have green and red in their bills too. With a bill that big, might the toucan tip over? It does not tip over because the bill is light. It is **hollow** and feels like a dry sponge. The bill has "teeth" built into the edges. The teeth let the toucan eat many different foods. Toucans enjoy fruit, tree frogs, and other birds' eggs!

Why is the toucan's bill so big? Some scientists think that the big bill scares away **enemies**. Other scientists think that it helps the bird get food from the ends of branches. And, some scientists say that the huge bill has no special use at all.

The toucan also has strange feet. It has four toes. Two toes face forward; two toes face backward. This helps the bird hold onto wet branches in the rain forest.

Another strange thing about the toucan is its "feather" tongue. The bird has bristles on the end of its tongue. These are sharp little hairs. They help the bird make its loud, croaking call. In the rain forest, you can hear a toucan that is far away!

Toucans are friendly birds. They live in **flocks** of six or more birds. They look for homes in hollow trees. Then, they all sleep together in one big nest inside the tree. Both parents sit on the eggs. Both parents feed the chicks.

You do not have to visit the rain forest to see a toucan. The toucan's friendly nature makes it easy to tame. No wonder so many toucans live in zoos!

bill: a bird's mouth, also called a beak
hollow: empty inside
enemy: someone or something harmful or destructive
flock: a group of animals or people

Biggest Bill on the Block

Have you ever seen a toucan? It is a difficult bird to ignore! Just take a look at its head! A toucan's enormous **bill** is one-third the size of its entire body. Its vivid bill is colored yellow, orange, and black and, sometimes, even green and red. With such a massive bill, might the toucan topple over? It does not topple over because its bill is so light. It is actually **hollow**. It feels like a dry sponge. The bill has "teeth" built into the edges that allow the toucan to eat many different foods, including fruit, tree frogs, and even other birds' eggs!

But, why is the toucan's bill so huge? Some scientists think that the bill scares away **enemies**. Other scientists think that it helps the bird reach food from the ends of branches. And, some scientists say that the bill has no special use at all.

The toucan also has peculiar feet. What would it be like to have toes growing out of your heels? Ask a toucan! It has two toes that face forward and two more that face backward. These strange feet help the toucan keep a tight grip on wet branches in the rain forest.

Another interesting thing about the toucan is its "feather" tongue. The toucan has bristles, or sharp little hairs, on the end of its tongue. This helps the bird make its loud, croaking call. In the rain forest, you can hear a toucan's call from far away!

Toucans are sociable. They live in **flocks** of six or more birds. They search for homes in hollow trees. Then, they all sleep together in one large nest inside the tree. When toucans have babies, both parents sit on the eggs and feed the chicks. The toucan's pleasant nature makes it easy to tame. That is why toucans at the zoo are so friendly.

bill: a bird's mouth, also called a beak
hollow: empty inside
enemy: someone or something harmful or destructive
flock: a group of animals or people

● ○ ○

Biggest Bill on the Block

Answer the questions.

1. What is one of the toucan's most interesting features?

A. its small bill

B. its soft, lovely song

C. its five-toed feet

D. none of the above

2. What part of a toucan is yellow, orange, and black?

A. wing **B.** head **C.** bill **D.** toe

3. Choose the best description of the toucan.

A. a friendly bird with funny feet

B. a large-billed rain forest bird that lives in groups

C. a small black bird that eats leaves

D. a rain forest bird

4. What are *bristles*? Write your answer in a complete sentence.

_____

_____

5. Write three words or phrases from the story to tell about the toucan's bill.

A. _____

B. _____

C. _____

6. Circle four adjectives that describe the toucan.

slow friendly loud

fierce meat-eating big-billed

7. The toucan makes its home, or nest, inside a hollow tree. Other animals make their homes in different places. Think of two other animals. Can you describe their homes? Why do you think they chose these types of homes? Write a short paragraph on another sheet of paper. Use complete sentences. Share your writing with a classmate. How do your paragraphs compare with each other? Revise your work.

Quiet, I Am Sleeping

We sleep about eight hours at a time. The three-toed sloth sleeps almost 20 hours. We are awake in the day. The sloth is awake at night. This is when the sloth eats. The three-toed sloth lives in trees. It eats leaves. Sometimes, it moves to another tree. Then, it eats more leaves. And, then it nods off again!

The sloth is not lazy. It is saving energy. Sleeping saves energy. Moving slowly saves energy too.

The sloth lives in the **rain forest**. It stays high up in the trees. This keeps it safe. Most enemies cannot reach it. But, large snakes will sometimes attack the sloth. Big birds may too.

Sometimes, the sloth climbs down. The sloth has sharp **claws**. It can use these to fight. But, it moves very slowly. This makes the sloth easy to catch. There is more danger on the ground. So, it **seldom** leaves the trees. Sloths live in Central and South America. They do not seem afraid of people. They often live near villages.

Sloths are very still. They are very quiet. People used to think that a sloth stayed in one tree forever! This is not true. The sloth has to eat. It has to change trees to find more leaves. Sloths move. They just move very slowly.

If a sloth is not climbing, it is hanging. It hangs upside down. Its feet **grip** a tree branch. Its body hangs below its feet. The sloth spends most of its life this way. It sleeps upside down. It eats upside down. The sloth is SLeepy. It is SLow. Maybe that is why it is called a SLoth!

rain forest: a thick forest where it rains a lot
claws: an animal's sharp nails
seldom: hardly ever
grip: to hold tightly

Quiet, I Am Sleeping

We sleep about eight hours each night. The three-toed sloth sleeps 15 to 20 hours a day. The sloth lives in the trees. It is more awake at night. That is when it eats leaves. Sometimes, the sloth moves slowly to the next tree. Then, it eats more leaves. And, sometimes while it is eating, the sloth nods off again!

The sloth is not lazy. It is just saving energy. Sleeping saves energy. Moving slowly saves energy too.

The sloth lives in the **rain forest**. It sleeps and eats high up in the trees. This keeps it safe. Most enemies cannot reach it. But, large snakes will sometimes attack the sloth. Big birds may too.

Sometimes, the sloth climbs down. The sloth has long, sharp **claws**. It can fight with these claws. But, it moves very slowly. Sloths are easy to catch. There is more danger on the ground. So, the sloth only climbs down about once a week. Sloths live in Central and South America. They do not seem afraid of humans and often live near villages.

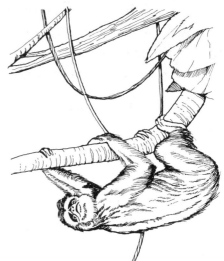

Sloths are very still and very quiet. Scientists used to think that a sloth stayed in one tree for its whole life! This is not true. The sloth eats leaves. It has to change trees to eat more leaves.

When the sloth is not climbing, it is hanging upside down. It grips a tree branch by its feet. The sloth spends most of its life this way. This is how it sleeps and eats. Maybe this is why its **organs**, including its **stomach**, are in different places than in other animals. This is just one more difference in this slow, snoozing animal.

---

rain forest: a thick forest where it rains a lot
claws: an animal's sharp nails
organ: a body part that performs a special job
stomach: a body part where food is broken down

Quiet, I Am Sleeping

Adult humans sleep about eight hours each night. The three-toed sloth sleeps at least twice that long. A sloth needs 15 to 20 hours of sleep a day. The three-toed sloth lives in trees. When it wakes up at night, it has a busy life. It eats leaves. Sometimes, it moves slowly to the next tree and eats more leaves. And, sometimes while it is eating, the sloth nods off again!

The sloth is not lazy. Its life of sleeping and slow moves lets it save energy. In the **rain forest**, the sloth sleeps and eats high up in the trees. This keeps it safe from most of its enemies. However, large snakes and big birds will sometimes attack the sloth in the trees. Most other animals cannot reach it there.

When it comes down to the ground, the sloth is in constant danger. The sloth has long, sharp **claws** to use if it has to fight. But, it moves very slowly and is easy to catch. Because of this risk, the sloth only climbs down from the treetops about once a week. Sloths live in Central and South America. They do not seem afraid of humans and often live near villages.

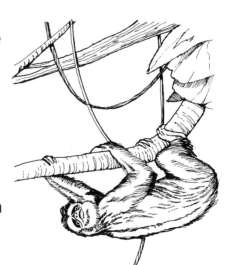

Sloths are so still and quiet that scientists used to think that they stayed in one tree for their whole lives! This is not true. The sloth climbs from one tree to another so that it can keep eating leaves.

The sloth spends the rest of its time upside down. It hangs from branches by its feet. The sloth sleeps and eats upside down. Because it spends so much time like this, some of its **organs**—its liver, **stomach**, and spleen—are in different places than in other animals. This is just one more difference in this strangely different, snoozing animal.

rain forest: a thick forest where it rains every day
claws: an animal's sharp nails
organ: a body part that performs a special job
stomach: a body part where food is broken down

Quiet, I Am Sleeping

Answer the questions.

Match each word to its antonym.

1. _____ climbs   **A.** defend

2. _____ attack   **B.** safety

3. _____ upside down   **C.** quickly

4. _____ danger   **D.** falls

5. _____ slowly   **E.** upright

6. Reread the last sentence in the first paragraph. What is a synonym for *nods off*?

   A. agrees   **B.** eats up   **C.** falls asleep   **D.** wakes up

7. Finish these sentences.

   A. The sloth sleeps so much _____ .

   B. The sloth spends a lot of its life hanging _____ .

   C. Two of the sloth's enemies are _____ and _____ .

8. Circle the correct word or phrase in parentheses to complete each sentence.

   A. The sloth (does, does not) seem to be afraid of humans.

   B. The sloth needs to sleep about (8, 20, 30) hours a day.

   C. The sloth eats during the (day, night).

   D. The sloth uses its sharp (teeth, toes, claws) if it needs to fight.

9. The sloth stays up in the trees for most of its life. Give two reasons why.

   _____

   _____

10. According to the story, the three-toed sloth often lives near villages. What do you think this tells you about the sloth? Explain why you think this way. Write a short paragraph on another sheet of paper. Use complete sentences.

Talk to Me

We are **mammals**. The **bottlenose dolphin** is a mammal too. We breathe air. The dolphin does too. We live in groups. The dolphin does too. Our groups are called families. Dolphin family groups are called pods. We can talk. We use **language**. What about dolphins?

Do dolphins have "words" for things? Can they tell each other thoughts? If they do, then they use language too. We know that dolphins make sounds. They make hundreds of different noises. We cannot understand these noises. But, maybe other dolphins can. Do these sounds have meaning?

Every bottlenose dolphin can whistle. Each whistle is different. This is called a signature whistle. Scientists think this whistle is like a name. What does it tell other dolphins? Maybe it says: "I am me. I am from this pod. I am from this father and mother. Right now, I am happy (or sad or scared)."

Dolphins do not just whistle. They use many other sounds too. They buzz. They yell. They scream. They even make a noise like a motorbike. We make sounds using our mouths. A dolphin makes sounds using its blowhole. What is a blowhole? It is a hole on top of the dolphin's head.

Humans "talk" in other ways. We smile. We frown. Bottlenose dolphins "talk" in other ways too. They use their bodies. They kick with their tails. They roll their eyes. They rub against other dolphins. Sometimes, two dolphins swim side by side. Then, they touch **fins**. It seems as if they are holding hands.

Scientists hope to learn more about dolphins. Why? They want to find out if the bottlenose dolphin really uses language. Then, scientists will be able to answer the question: "Can dolphins talk?"

mammal: a warm-blooded animal with bones and hair or fur
bottlenose dolphin: a smart, long-nosed whale with teeth
language: communication through sound or symbols
fin: a part of an animal used to help it swim

Talk to Me

We are **mammals**. The **bottlenose dolphin** is a mammal too. We breathe air. The dolphin does too. We live in groups. The dolphin does too. Our groups are called families. The dolphin's family is called a pod. We use **language**. We can talk. Can dolphins talk too?

Do dolphins have their own language? Scientists do not know. If dolphins did, they would have "words" for things. They would be able to tell each other whole thoughts. Dolphins make sounds. We can hear these noises. Scientists have counted over 1,700 different dolphin sounds. These sounds were made within one group of dolphins.

Every bottlenose dolphin can whistle. Each whistle is different. Scientists think a dolphin's whistle is like a name. They call this a signature whistle. What does a signature whistle tell other dolphins? Maybe something like this: "I am me, from this pod. Right now, I am happy (or sad or scared)."

Dolphins use many other sounds too. They make a buzzing noise. They make sounds like a yell or scream. They even make a noise that sounds like a motorbike. We make sounds using our mouths. A dolphin makes sounds using its blowhole. A blowhole is a hole on top of the dolphin's head.

Bottlenose dolphins "talk" in other ways too. They do not just use sound. They use their bodies. They kick with their tails. They roll their eyes. They brush against other dolphins. Sometimes, two dolphins swim side by side. Then, they touch **fins**. It seems as if they are holding hands.

Scientists hope to learn more about dolphins. Why? They want to discover if the bottlenose dolphin has a real language! Then, scientists will be able to answer the question: "Can dolphins talk?"

mammal: a warm-blooded animal with bones and hair or fur
bottlenose dolphin: a smart, long-nosed whale with teeth
language: communication through sound or symbols
fin: a part of an animal used to help it swim

Talk to Me

The **bottlenose dolphin** is a **mammal**, just like us. It breathes air like we do. It lives in family groups, called pods. But, can the dolphin also talk like we can?

Scientists do not know if dolphins have their own **language**. If they did, then dolphins would have "words" for different things. It would mean that they could tell each other whole thoughts. We do know it is true that dolphins make hundreds of sounds. Some scientists have counted over 1,700 different sounds made within one group of dolphins.

Every bottlenose dolphin has a whistle that is its very own, like a name. Scientists call this a signature whistle. They think that it means something like this: "I am me, from this pod and from this father and mother. Right now, I am happy (or sad or scared)."

Dolphins use many other sounds too. They make a buzzing noise. They yell and scream and even make a noise that sounds like a motorbike. None of these sounds come from a dolphin's mouth. The dolphin uses a blowhole on top of its head to make these sounds.

Bottlenose dolphins "talk" in other ways too. They use their bodies to speak. Dolphins kick with their tails and roll their eyes. They brush against other dolphins. Sometimes, two dolphins swim side by side and touch **fins**, as if they are holding hands.

Someday, scientists hope to know more about dolphin sounds. They want to know if the bottlenose dolphin has a real language or not. Then, they will be able to answer the question: "Can dolphins talk?"

bottlenose dolphin: a smart, long-nosed whale with teeth
mammal: a warm-blooded animal with bones and hair or fur
language: communication through sound or symbols
fin: a part of an animal used to help it swim

Talk to Me

Answer the questions.

1. Bottlenose dolphins do not just make sounds. They "talk" in other ways too. What is a possible name for this way of talking?

    A. motorbike speech   **B.** body language

    C. mind reading   **D.** swim talk

2. Which definition of *pod* is used in the story?

    A. common term for a group of offices   **B.** a seed and its covering

    C. a family group   **D.** none of the above

3. According to the story, what do you think is the main difference between animal sounds and a language?

    A. All animals that make sound have a language.

    B. Language means more than a series of calls or cries.

    C. Language means that each animal has its own call.

    D. Animals like dolphins definitely have a language.

4. What do you think the author's main purpose was in writing this story? Write your answer in one or two complete sentences.

_____

_____

5. Which of the following dolphin sounds is not listed in the story?

    A. whistle   **B.** yell   **C.** motorbike sound   **D.** bark

Write **T** for true or **F** for false.

6. _____ Dolphins use their mouths to make their calls.

7. _____ Sometimes dolphins touch fins as they swim.

8. _____ Dolphins are fish.

9. _____ Scientists have heard about 20 different dolphin sounds.

10. Describe two ways that the bottlenose dolphin uses its body to talk. Write your answer in complete sentences on another sheet of paper. Show your answer to your teacher. Revise your work if necessary.

Honest Abe's Return

Ghosts! Do they scare you? Try sleeping at the **White House**. This famous American house seems to be haunted. Many people say a ghost lives there. Whose ghost? It is President **Abraham Lincoln**'s!

White House workers say they have seen Lincoln's ghost many times. They say that strange things happen. Doors close. Lights turn on. But, nobody is there! One man said he saw a person sitting outside of Lincoln's old office. The person looked like President Lincoln! Was it a ghost?

Important people visit the White House. Some say that they have seen this ghost. Lincoln's office is now a bedroom. It is called the "Lincoln Bedroom." This is where the ghost is seen the most.

Queen Wilhelmina of **the Netherlands** once stayed here. She heard a knock. She opened the door. Lincoln's ghost was there! The queen **fainted**.

Winston Churchill was a famous British leader. He also said he saw the ghost. Churchill was visiting the White House. He walked into the Lincoln Bedroom. Lincoln was standing inside!

A First Lady has seen Lincoln's ghost too. Grace Coolidge said she saw Lincoln. He was looking out the window. Mrs. Coolidge thought he looked sad.

Have animals seen this ghost too? President Reagan's dog stopped at the door to the Lincoln Bedroom. Then, it barked. It did not even go inside!

You can read about Lincoln's ghost on a White House website. There, people tell ghost stories. These people say that they have seen President Lincoln . . . more than 100 years after his death.

White House: the home of the president of the United States
Abraham Lincoln: the 16th president of the United States (1861–1865)
The Netherlands: a country in northwestern Europe, also called Holland
faint: to pass out, sometimes from fear or shock

2.RI.4, 2.RI.10, 2.RF.4, 2.L.4

Honest Abe's Return

Do ghosts frighten you? Try sleeping at the **White House**. You may end up terrified! This famous American house seems to be haunted. Who is the White House's most famous ghost? It's President **Abraham Lincoln**!

White House workers say they have seen Lincoln's ghost many times. One man said he saw Lincoln sitting outside of a room that had been his office. Workers say they have seen doors close by themselves. Lights turn on by themselves. Some workers think this could be Lincoln's ghost at work.

Many important people visit the White House. Some also say that they have seen this ghost. Lincoln's office has been converted into a bedroom. It is called the "Lincoln Bedroom." This is where the ghost is seen the most.

Queen Wilhelmina of **the Netherlands** once stayed in the White House. She heard a knock at the door. Lincoln's ghost was there! She **fainted**.

Winston Churchill was a famous British leader. He also said he saw the ghost. Churchill was visiting the White House. He walked into the Lincoln Bedroom to find Lincoln standing inside!

One First Lady, Grace Coolidge, said that she saw Lincoln there too. He was looking out the window. Mrs. Coolidge thought he looked sad.

Animals may have seen this ghost. President Reagan's dog stopped at the door to the Lincoln Bedroom. Then, it barked. It did not even go inside!

A White House website talks about Lincoln's ghost. People tell ghost stories. These people all say that they have seen President Lincoln . . . more than 100 years after his death.

White House: the home of the president of the United States
Abraham Lincoln: the 16th president of the United States (1861–1865)
The Netherlands: a country in northwestern Europe, also called Holland
faint: to pass out, sometimes from fear or shock

Honest Abe's Return

Do you believe in ghosts? If you ever spent the night at the **White House**, you might. This famous American house seems to be haunted. And, who do you think is its most famous ghost? It's President **Abraham Lincoln**!

People who work at the White House say they have seen Lincoln's ghost many times. One man said he saw Lincoln sitting outside of a room that used to be his office. Workers say they have also seen doors close all by themselves. Lights turn on by themselves near this room. The workers think that the ghost of President Lincoln could be doing these things.

Other people claim to have seen Lincoln's ghost too. Queen Wilhelmina of **the Netherlands** once visited the White House. She heard a knock at the door. When she saw Lincoln's ghost there, the queen **fainted**!

A famous British leader, Sir Winston Churchill, also said he saw the ghost. Lincoln's office was later converted into a bedroom. Churchill stayed there. He walked into the bedroom. There was Lincoln, standing right next to the fireplace.

The ghost is seen most frequently in the "Lincoln Bedroom." First Lady Grace Coolidge said that she saw Lincoln there. She said that he was gazing out the window, and he looked sad. President Reagan's dog would not even go into the Lincoln Bedroom. The dog just stood at the door and barked!

A White House website shares puzzling stories about Lincoln's ghost. People tell tales about the ghost. These people all say that they have seen President Lincoln's ghost . . . more than 100 years after his death.

White House: the home of the president of the United States
Abraham Lincoln: the 16th president of the United States (1861–1865)
The Netherlands: a country in northwestern Europe, also called Holland
faint: to pass out, sometimes from fear or shock

2.RI.1, 2.W.1, 2.W.5, 2.L.1, 2.L.4

Honest Abe's Return

Answer the questions.

1. Grace Coolidge was a First Lady. What is a *First Lady*?

    A. a female president

    B. the first woman who lived in the White House

    C. the wife of a president

    D. the daughter of a president

2. The ghost of President Lincoln is said to haunt

    A. the White House.

    B. his former office.

    C. the Lincoln Bedroom.

    D. all of the above

Match each word to its synonym.

3. _____ scare   **A.** tales

4. _____ seems   **B.** frighten

5. _____ stories   **C.** appears

6. Which of the following is not in the story?

    A. how Abraham Lincoln died

    B. where Winston Churchill said he saw the ghost

    C. how President Reagan's dog acted outside the Lincoln Bedroom

    D. which First Lady thought she saw the ghost

7. Which of the following best states the main idea of the story?

    A. Many people have told stories about seeing the ghost of Lincoln in the White House.

    B. The queen of the Netherlands fainted when she thought she saw the ghost.

    C. Dogs do not like ghosts.

    D. Lincoln ghost stories may or may not be true.

8. Look at the sentence. Circle *do* or *do not*. Then, write the reason for your answer in the form of a letter to a friend on another sheet of paper. Use complete sentences in your paragraph. Remember to use correct greeting and closing punctuation.

I (do, do not) believe in ghosts.

The Ink Monkey

There are many Chinese stories about monkeys. The stories are from long ago. Some monkeys were very small. One weighed just seven ounces (198.45 g). These monkeys were smart. People trained them. This is one of the stories.

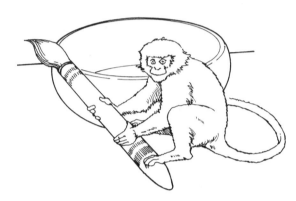

*Once there lived a man named Zhu Xi. He was a famous **thinker**. He had a tiny "ink monkey" for a pet. It sat on his desk. It handed him pens. It helped him make ink.*

How could a monkey sleep in a paintbrush pot? That is so small! How could a monkey learn to make ink? That is so smart! It was just a story! It had to be fiction!

Dan Gebo is an American **scientist**. In 2000, he discovered some bones. The bones were in China. They were from a very old monkey. This monkey was small. It was the size of a mouse. Some foot bones were very small. They looked like **grains** of rice! Gebo says that this monkey may be a missing link. A missing link is an animal. It is important. It can tell us more about how humans grew. Gebo named his find "the dawn monkey."

Is the dawn monkey related to the ink monkey? Is the dawn monkey its **ancestor**? The dawn monkey is small. It is smaller than we thought monkeys could be. So, we know that a tiny Chinese monkey did exist. Could this be related to Zhu Xi's pet?

After Dr. Gebo's find came another shock. The Chinese said that they had found an ink monkey. A living ink monkey! It was found in a forest. Zhu Xi once lived near this forest! But, the Chinese have not said anything more.

thinker: someone who spends a lot of time thinking, or meditating
scientist: someone who studies science
grain: a small seed or tiny single piece
ancestor: an earlier relative

The Ink Monkey

There are many Chinese stories about monkeys. The stories are from long ago. Some monkeys were very small. One weighed just seven ounces (198.45 g). These monkeys were also smart. They were so smart that people trained them. This is one of the stories.

*Years ago, there lived a man named Zhu Xi. He was a famous **thinker**. He had a tiny "ink monkey" for a pet. It sat on his desk. It handed him pens. It helped him make ink.*

How could a monkey sleep in a paintbrush pot? That was so small! How could a monkey learn to make ink? That was so smart! It was just a story! It had to be fiction!

In 2000, an American **scientist** discovered some bones. They were from a very old monkey. The bones were found in China. This monkey was small, like a mouse. Some foot bones were as tiny as a **grain** of rice! The scientist, Dan Gebo, says that this monkey may be a missing link. A missing link is important. It is an animal that can tell us more about how humans **evolved**. Gebo calls his find "the dawn monkey."

Is the dawn monkey related to the ink monkey? Is the dawn monkey its ancestor? The dawn monkey is very small. It is much smaller than we thought monkeys could be. So, we know that a tiny Chinese monkey did exist. Could this be related to Zhu Xi's pet?

After Dr. Gebo's discovery came another surprise. The Chinese said that they had found a living ink monkey! It was found in a forest. Zhu Xi once lived near this very forest! But, the Chinese have not said anything more.

thinker: someone who spends a lot of time thinking, or meditating
scientist: someone who studies science
grain: a small seed or tiny single piece
evolve: to change very slowly

The Ink Monkey

In China, there are stories about tiny monkeys that lived long ago. Each creature weighed only seven ounces (198.45 g). The stories say that these monkeys were extremely smart. They were so smart that people trained them to do chores. Children in China tell stories about "the ink monkey." The ink monkey was the pet of a famous **thinker** named Zhu Xi. It sat on his desk and handed him pens when he was writing. It helped him make ink.

For hundreds of years, people thought that the story about the ink monkey was just a story. Think about a monkey so small that it could sleep in a paintbrush pot! Picture an animal so smart that it could learn to make ink! It had to be fiction!

But, in 2000, an American **scientist** discovered the bones of an **ancient** monkey. He made his discovery in China. This monkey had been as small as a mouse. It was so tiny that the bones in its feet were as small as grains of rice. The scientist, Dan Gebo, says that this monkey may be a missing link. This is an animal that can tell us more about how humans **evolved**. Gebo calls his find "the dawn monkey."

Could the dawn monkey be linked to the ink monkey? The dawn monkey is much smaller than we thought monkeys could ever be. Now, we know that millions of years ago, there really was a mouse-sized monkey living in China. Could the dawn monkey be the ancestor of Zhu Xi's pet?

Soon after Dr. Gebo's important discovery came another surprise. The Chinese said that they had found a living ink monkey! They said it was found in the forest where Zhu Xi once lived. But, the Chinese have not yet let other scientists know more.

thinker: someone who spends a lot of time thinking, or meditating
scientist: someone who studies science
ancient: extremely old
evolve: to change very slowly

The Ink Monkey

Answer the questions.

Match each word to its antonym.

1. _____ tiny
2. _____ discovered
3. _____ living
4. _____ handed

A. dead
B. took
C. huge
D. unknown

5. The "ink monkey" was the pet of

A. Dan Gebo.
B. Li Xi.
C. the dawn monkey.
D. Zhu Xi.

6. In the old Chinese story of the ink monkey, the monkey learns how to make ink. The author uses the phrase "*It had to be fiction!*" to describe this story. What is another way of saying this?

A. It had to be a discovery.
B. It had to be just a story.
C. It had to be true.
D. It had to be factual.

7. An animal that helps us understand how humans grew and evolved is

called a _____ _____.

8. Two different people are named in this story. Who are they, and what did they do? Write your answers in complete sentences on another sheet of paper. Please use correct capitalization and punctuation.

9. The "dawn monkey" was the size of

A. a grain of rice.
B. a squirrel.
C. a mouse.
D. a pen.

10. Do you believe there was an ink monkey, or do you think the story is fiction? Why do you think so? Type a short paragraph into a computer. Use complete sentences. Then, share your work with a friend. How does your work compare with your friend's writing?

Sweet Machines

Doughnuts have been a treat for hundreds of years. The **Dutch** first made them as "oily cakes." Dough balls were rolled by hand. They were dropped one by one into a kettle of hot oil. Dutch cooks filled the cakes with sweets such as raisins or jam. Each doughnut was made by hand.

Today, doughnut machines make thousands of doughnuts at once. How do machines make so many?

One machine makes the doughnuts round. Then, a moving belt carries them away. The first stop is a warming oven. Doughnuts contain **yeast**. Heat makes yeast puff up. The oven makes the doughnuts puffy too. After the dough rises, the doughnuts ride on. The next stop is an oil bath. The doughnuts **fry** in the hot oil. Then, they land back on the belt.

Some belts flip the doughnuts over. These doughnuts cook on both sides. Some machines spray hot oil over the doughnuts. This cooks the tops.

Some doughnuts have a sugary topping made from sugar and milk. This is called a glaze. These doughnuts go for a ride through a waterfall of glaze! The glaze coats the doughnuts.

Do you like frosted doughnuts? Frosted doughnuts are dipped in flavored frosting.

Some doughnuts still have fillings. The fillings can be cream or jam. These doughnuts ride to another machine. Someone pushes each doughnut against a pipe. The pipe pumps filling into the doughnut.

What is the last stop on this sweet ride? You guessed it! Doughnut boxes!

Dutch: people from the Netherlands, or Holland

yeast: a powder made from fungus that makes dough rise

fry: to cook in very hot oil or fat

Sweet Machines

Doughnuts have been a sweet treat for centuries. The **Dutch** first made them as "oily cakes." Small dough balls were rolled carefully by hand. They were dropped one by one into a kettle of oil. But, they did not cook all of the way through. So, Dutch cooks filled the cakes with raisins or jam.

Today, doughnut machines make thousands of doughnuts at one time. How do machines make so many of these sweet treats?

One machine stamps out, or shapes, doughnuts into their round shape. A moving belt carries them into a warming oven. Doughnuts contain **yeast**. Heat makes yeast puff up. The warm oven makes the doughnuts puff up. Then, the doughnuts continue on their journey. They plop into a big bath. This is not a water bath. It is an oil bath! The doughnuts **fry** in the hot oil. When they are cooked, they land back on the belt.

Some belts flip the doughnuts over. These doughnuts cook on both sides. Some machines spray hot oil over the doughnuts. This cooks the tops.

Some doughnuts have a sugary topping that is a clear sheet of sugar and milk. These doughnuts ride through a waterfall of glaze! The glaze coats the doughnuts.

Frosted doughnuts are dipped in flavored frosting before they finish their ride.

Some doughnuts still have fillings such as cream or jam. At another machine, someone pushes each doughnut against a pipe. The pipe pumps delicious filling into the doughnut.

What is the last stop on this long, tasty ride? You guessed it! Doughnut boxes!

Dutch: people from the Netherlands, or Holland
yeast: a powder made from fungus that makes dough rise
fry: to cook in very hot oil or fat

Sweet Machines

Doughnuts have been a favorite dessert for hundreds of years. The **Dutch** first made these "oily cakes." Little balls of dough were rolled by hand. They were dropped into a boiling kettle of oil. Dutch cooks filled the little cakes with raisins or jam. Each doughnut was handmade.

Today, doughnut machines make thousands of the treats at one time. How do machines make so many of these sweet treats?

One machine stamps out, or shapes, doughnuts into their round shape. Then, the doughnuts ride on a moving belt. First, the belt carries the doughnuts into a warming oven that makes the **yeast** in the dough puff up. Then, they get dumped into an oil bath where they are **fried**. The doughnuts float in the hot oil and, once they are cooked, they land back on the belt. On some machines, the doughnuts are flipped so both sides are cooked. Other machines spray hot oil over them to cook the tops.

The ride is not finished yet. Doughnuts usually have some kind of sugar coating. Some doughnuts are glazed with a clear sheet of sugar and milk. These doughnuts go for a ride through a waterfall of glaze! The sheet of glaze coats the doughnuts.

Other doughnuts are filled with **gooey** cream or jam, as they were centuries ago. These doughnuts ride to another machine. Someone pushes each doughnut against a pipe that pumps filling into the doughnut. Frosted doughnuts are dipped in vanilla or chocolate frosting before they ride out on the belt.

And the final stop? Boxes filled to the brim with delicious doughnuts!

Dutch: people from the Netherlands, or Holland
yeast: a powder made from fungus that makes dough rise
fried: cooked in very hot oil or fat
gooey: wet and sticky

Sweet Machines

Answer the questions.

1. Which of the following sentences is an opinion?

    A. The Dutch invented doughnuts.
    B. Doughnuts are the best breakfast treat of all time.
    C. Today, most doughnuts are made by machines.
    D. Doughnuts ride on belts as they are cooked and frosted.

2. Doughnuts contain yeast. Yeast is what makes the dough puff up, or rise. Can you think of another type of food that has to rise before it is cooked?

    A. steak   **B.** butter   **C.** salad   **D.** bread

3. What is *glaze*?

    A. a mixture of sugar and candy
    B. a mixture of yeast and milk
    C. a mixture of frosting and jam
    D. a mixture of sugar and milk

4. Which of the following is not a step in doughnut making?

    A. rising in a warming oven   **B.** floating in an oil bath
    C. hanging on lines to dry   **D.** shaping dough to make it round

Match each word to its antonym.

5. _____ filled   **A.** emptied

6. _____ treat   **B.** fall

7. _____ rise   **C.** necessity

8. Write down the names of two companies or stores that make doughnuts or other baked goods. Make sure you use correct capitalization.

_____

_____

9. Do you like doughnuts? Why or why not? Write a short paragraph on another sheet of paper. Use complete sentences.

A Wild Ride

A roller coaster plunges down hills. It races around turns. It is exciting! And, it is mostly run by nature!

A **machine** pulls the roller coaster cars up the first hill. This is the lift hill. On simple roller coasters, the machine is like a **towrope**. Chains pull the cars up this hill. Then, the chains are released. Gravity pulls the cars down. When it heads up another hill, gravity slows the roller coaster's tail end. That is why it slows down and speeds up during the ride.

Most roller coaster rides have hills that get smaller. The biggest hill is usually the lift hill. This makes energy for the rest of the ride! As the roller coaster zooms over smaller hills, it slows. Finally, it coasts to a stop.

There are two kinds of roller coasters. Older roller coasters are wooden. Their tracks are like train tracks. The tracks rattle. The cars sway from side to side. This makes these rides fun. But, wood is hard to bend. So, it is hard to make a twisty wooden roller coaster. Most of the thrill comes from lots of hills.

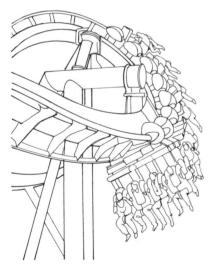

Newer roller coasters are made of **steel**. Some run on tracks, like a train. Others run on rails, like a **subway**. Steel tracks are easier to bend. These roller coasters have more turns. The cars can even flip upside down! The tracks are made in big chunks. They look like pieces of a skyscraper. They are put together using very few joints. This makes the ride smooth. Two sets of wheels keep the cars on the tracks.

With thrilling twists, turns, and drops, it is no wonder that people love roller coasters!

machine: something with moving and fixed parts that does work
towrope: a rope or chain used to pull large objects
steel: a very strong metal
subway: an underground railway, usually found in large cities

A Wild Ride

A roller coaster plunges down hills. It races around corners. It is exciting! And it is mostly run by nature!

A **machine** pulls the roller coaster cars up the first hill. On simple roller coasters, the machine is like a **towrope**. Chains help pull the cars up this hill, called the lift hill. Then, the chains are released. Gravity pulls the roller coaster down the hill. When it heads up another hill, gravity slows the roller coaster's tail end. That is why it slows down and speeds up during the ride.

Many roller coasters are built with hills that become smaller and smaller. The biggest hill is almost always the lift hill. This creates a lot of energy for the rest of the ride! As the roller coaster zooms over smaller hills, it starts to slow. Finally, it coasts to a stop.

There are two kinds of roller coasters. Older roller coasters are wooden. Their tracks are like train tracks. Part of the fun of these roller coasters is the way the tracks rattle. The cars sway from side to side. But, wood is hard to bend. It is hard to make a wooden roller coaster with many twists and turns. Most of the thrill comes from lots of hills.

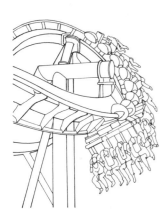

Newer roller coasters are made of **steel**. Some run on tracks, like a train. Others run on rails, like a **subway**. Steel tracks are easier to bend. Steel roller coasters have more turns. Sometimes, the cars even flip upside down! Steel tracks are made in huge chunks that look like skyscraper pieces. The tracks are put together using very few joints. This makes the ride speedy and smooth. Two sets of wheels keep the cars from running off the tracks.

With thrilling twists, turns, and drops, it is no wonder that people love roller coasters!

machine: something with moving and fixed parts that does work
towrope: a rope or chain used to pull large objects
steel: a very strong metal
subway: an underground railway, usually found in large cities

A Wild Ride

A roller coaster plunges down hills and races around corners. It is incredibly exciting! And, it is mostly run by nature!

A **machine** pulls the roller coaster cars up the first hill. On simple roller coasters, the machine is like a **towrope**. Chains help pull the cars up this hill, called the lift hill. When, the chains are released, gravity pulls the roller coaster down the hill. When it heads up another hill, gravity slows the roller coaster's tail end. That is why it slows down and speeds up during the ride.

Many roller coasters are built with hills that become increasingly smaller. The biggest hill is usually the lift hill. This creates plenty of energy for the rest of the ride! As the roller coaster zooms over the smaller hills, it starts to slow. Finally, it coasts to a stop.

There are two kinds of roller coasters. Older roller coasters are wooden and have tracks like train tracks. Part of the excitement of wooden roller coasters is the way the tracks rattle and the cars sway from side to side. But, wood is difficult to bend. It is tricky to make a wooden roller coaster with many twists and turns. Most of the excitement comes from lots of hills.

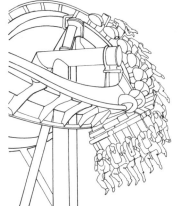

Newer roller coasters are made of **steel**. They can run on tracks, like a train, or on rails, like a **subway**. Steel tracks are easier to bend, so these roller coasters include more turns. Sometimes, the cars even flip upside down! Steel tracks are made in enormous sections that resemble skyscraper pieces. The tracks connect with very few joints. This makes the ride speedy and smooth. Two sets of wheels keep the cars from jumping off the tracks.

With thrilling twists, scary turns, and steep plunges, it is no wonder that people love roller coasters!

machine: something with moving and fixed parts that does work
towrope: a rope or chain used to pull large objects
steel: a very strong metal
subway: an underground railway, usually found in large cities

A Wild Ride

Answer the questions.

1. Why does the story say that roller coasters are *run by nature*?

    A. Roller coasters are natural objects.
    B. Roller coasters depend on gravity.
    C. Roller coasters are exciting.
    D. Roller coasters are built using natural objects.

2. The tracks on a wooden roller coaster are built like

    A. highway exits.   **B.** lift hills.   **C.** train tracks.   **D.** racetracks.

3. What does the word *coasts* mean as it is used in this sentence?

Finally, it coasts to a stop.

    A. places where the land meets the sea
    B. slowly stopping without brakes
    C. to travel past the side of something
    D. to race past something

4. What does the word *plunges* mean as it is used in this sentence?

A roller coaster plunges down hills.

    A. skates   **B.** dives   **C.** jumps   **D.** crawls

5. Describe the two main kinds of roller coasters in complete sentences.

_____

_____

6. What is another word for *joints*?

    A. seams   **B.** tracks   **C.** corners   **D.** twists

7. Which type of roller coaster do you think you would like better, steel or wooden? Why? Write your answer on another sheet of paper in the form of a letter to a friend. Ask your teacher to review it. Revise it if necessary. Remember to use complete sentences and a proper greeting and closing.

Mozart's Young Life

Some people learn slowly. Some learn quickly. And, some are born with **talent**. Wolfgang Amadeus Mozart had talent. Mozart was a musician. He made music. He was a **composer**. Mozart was even **famous** as a child!

Mozart always loved music. At three years old, he played the piano. He did not just bang on it. He played real songs! At five, Mozart wrote music. His father was a musician too. He and Mozart visited kings and queens. They went all over Europe. Mozart played in many cities. Sometimes, his father blindfolded him. Then, his father held him above the piano. Mozart hung upside down! He could not see! But, he still played perfectly! People were amazed!

At seven years old, Mozart started to publish his music. People could buy it. By age eight, Mozart played the organ. He also played the **violin**. Who taught Mozart? He did it himself! Mozart wrote more music too. He wrote a full-length piece. This is called a symphony. He wrote this when he was still young. At 13, Mozart wrote an opera. This musical work is like a play. The parts are not spoken. They are sung.

Mozart traveled a lot. He was not at home much. He was not really happy. Not everyone was as smart as he was. But, Mozart was not always smart. When he grew up, he spent too much money. He always needed more. Mozart died young. He was only 35 years old. But, people still play his music. It is still alive today.

---

talent: natural skill
composer: someone who writes music
famous: known by many people
violin: a musical instrument with four strings, played with a bow

Mozart's Young Life

Some people learn things slowly. Others are born with **talent**. Wolfgang Amadeus Mozart was born with talent. He made wonderful music. Mozart was a **famous composer**. He was even famous as a child!

At three years old, Mozart played the piano. He played real songs! At five, he wrote his own music. His father was a musician too. He took Mozart to visit kings and queens. Mozart played all over Europe. Sometimes, his father blindfolded young Mozart. Then, his father held him above the piano. Mozart was hanging upside down! He could not see the piano keys! But, he still played perfectly! Mozart amazed everyone who heard him.

At seven years old, Mozart started to publish his music. Now, other people could buy it. By eight, he could play the organ and **violin**. He taught himself! He also wrote longer music. He wrote a full-length piece. This is called a symphony. At 13, Mozart wrote his first opera. An opera is a musical work. It is like a play. But, the parts are not spoken. They are sung.

Mozart traveled a lot. He was not at home much. He was not really happy. Few people were as smart as he was. But, in other ways, Mozart was not smart. When he grew up, he spent too much money. He found it hard to make enough money. Mozart died young. He was only 35 years old. But, his music is still alive. It is played and loved all over the world.

talent: natural skill
famous: known by many people
composer: someone who writes music
violin: a musical instrument with four strings, played with a bow

Mozart's Young Life

Some people take a long time to learn new skills. Other people seem to be born with **talent**. That was true of Wolfgang Amadeus Mozart. When he was an adult, he was one of the most **famous** composers of all time. But, he was also brilliant as a small child.

When he was three years old, Mozart started to play songs on the piano. When he was five, he started to write his own music. His father was a musician too. He took the young Mozart on tours to the royal courts of kings and queens. Mozart played all over Europe. He could play perfectly, even when he was blindfolded and could not see the keys. His father held him over the piano, and the upside down boy could still play! He amazed the people who came to hear him.

Mozart started to publish his music when he was only seven years old. By the time he was eight, he had taught himself how to play the organ and the **violin**. He also wrote a symphony, a full-length piece of music. He was only 13 years old when he wrote his first opera. An opera is a work that is acted out like a play, with singing parts instead of speaking parts.

Because he traveled so much, Mozart was hardly ever at home. He was not really happy. Very few people were as smart as he was. But, in some ways, Mozart was not smart. He spent too much money. When he left his father and went to live on his own, he found it hard to make enough money. Mozart died when he was only 35 years old. His **works** are still played and loved all over the world today.

talent: natural skill
famous: known by many people
violin: a musical instrument with four strings, played with a bow
works: a collection of a person's creations

Mozart's Young Life

Answer the questions.

Match each word to its antonym.

1. _____ held   **A.** learned

2. _____ happy   **B.** ended

3. _____ taught   **C.** saved

4. _____ started   **D.** let go

5. _____ spent   **E.** sad

6. A compound word is a long word made up of two shorter words. Use the list of words to create three compound words.

child	every	him	hood	one
road	self	song	trip	writer

_____ _____ _____

7. Circle the correct word or phrase in parentheses to complete each of the following sentences.

    A. People (do, do not) play Mozart's music today.

    B. Mozart (was, was not) good at handling money.

    C. Mozart died when he was (23, 35, 48) years old.

8. What is an *opera*?

    A. a full-length piece of music
    B. a play with parts that are played silently
    C. a kind of game played at court
    D. a play with parts that are sung

9. How do you think Mozart could have had a happier life? Type a short paragraph on a computer. Use complete sentences. Share your work with your teacher. Then, revise your writing.

The Businessman

When Cameron Johnson was seven years old, his mother gave him some tomatoes. He wanted to sell them. He asked for one dollar each. A woman said that was too much. But, Cameron did not change his price. He thought someone else might pay a dollar.

Cameron knows how to sell things. When he was nine years old, he got his first computer. Did he play games? No. He set up his first business! He made special cards on his computer. Then, he sold them. He started selling things online. He sold his sister's toys. Then, he bought more toys. He sold them too. He sold 40 toys each day! Cameron made $50,000 that year. He was 12 years old.

How did Cameron learn how to do this? His family helped. His **great-grandfather** started as a car dealer. His father runs the **company** now. Cameron's parents talked to him about money. He learned how to save money. He learned how to keep track of it too.

Cameron is also a good writer. He writes well about the things that he sells. And, he has great ideas. Cameron does not just talk. He does things.

Cameron looks for ways to sell things too. His father needed help. He wanted to check lists of people who might want to buy cars. Cameron figured out how to use his computer to help. Now, he sells this **software** to other dealers.

You do not have to make a lot of money to be happy. That is what Cameron says. A business can be big or small. But, no one is too old to start a business. And, no one is too young!

great-grandfather: the father of a grandfather
company: a business that sells things
software: instructions used by a computer

The Businessman

When Cameron Johnson was seven years old, his mother gave him some tomatoes. He wanted to sell them. A woman asked him how much they were. He asked for one dollar each. The woman said that was too much. But, Cameron did not change his price. He knew that someone else might pay a dollar.

Cameron knows how to sell things. When he was nine years old, he got his first computer. Did he play computer games? No. He set up his first business! He made special cards on his computer. Then, he sold them. He started selling things online. He sold his sister's stuffed animals. He bought more stuffed animals. He sold them too. He was selling 40 animals each day! Cameron made $50,000 that year. He was 12 years old.

How did Cameron learn how to do this? His family helped. His **great-grandfather** started as a car dealer. His father runs the **company** today. Cameron's parents talked to him about money. He learned how to save his money. He learned how to keep track of it too.

Cameron is also a good writer. He writes well about the things that he sells. And, he has great ideas. Cameron acts instead of just talking about things.

Cameron also looks for ways to sell things. His father needed help in checking lists of people who might want to buy cars. Cameron figured out how to use his computer to help. Now, he sells his **software** to other people who sell cars.

Cameron says that you do not have to make a lot of money to be happy. Businesses can be big or small. No one is too old or too young to give business a try.

---

great-grandfather: the father of a grandfather
company: a business that sells things
software: instructions used by a computer

The Businessman

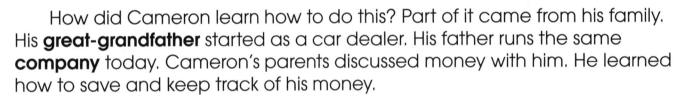

When Cameron Johnson was seven years old, he wanted to sell some tomatoes from the garden. A woman asked how much he was **charging** for one tomato. When he suggested a dollar, she said it was too much to pay. But, Cameron did not lower his price. He knew someone else might pay a dollar.

Cameron knows how to sell things. When he was nine years old, he received his very first computer. With it, he created his first business. He made special cards and envelopes on his computer and sold them. Then, he started selling his sister's stuffed animals online. Later, he bought more and sold them too. He sold 40 animals a day! Cameron made $50,000 that year. He was 12 years old.

How did Cameron learn how to do this? Part of it came from his family. His **great-grandfather** started as a car dealer. His father runs the same **company** today. Cameron's parents discussed money with him. He learned how to save and keep track of his money.

Cameron writes well about the things that he sells. And, he has terrific ideas. Cameron acts instead of just talking about his ideas.

Cameron is always on the lookout for chances to sell things too. His father needed help in checking lists of people who might want to buy cars. Cameron figured out how to use his computer to help. Now, he sells his **software** to other people who sell cars.

Cameron believes that you do not have to make a lot of money to be happy. Your business can be big or small. No one is too old or too young to give business a try.

---

charge: to ask a price for an item
great-grandfather: the father of a grandfather
company: a business that sells things
software: instructions used by a computer

The Businessman

Answer the questions.

1. Which phrase could replace *online*?

A. with software
B. over a phone line
C. on the Internet
D. none of the above

2. Which sentence is not written using the past tense of the verb?

A. Cameron said that a business can be small.
B. Cameron sold cards.
C. Cameron enjoys talking.
D. Cameron bought more toys.

3. Which adjective best describes Cameron Johnson?

A. smart **B.** lazy **C.** cautious **D.** careless

4. Why do you think the author put this information in the story?

Cameron made $50,000 that year. He was 12 years old.

A. To show that Cameron was a big success when he was still young
B. To show how good Cameron was at selling
C. To show that Cameron could have made more money
D. A. and B.

5. What is another word or phrase for *figured out* in this sentence?

Cameron figured out how to use his computer to help.

A. found out **B.** multiplied **C.** added up **D.** all of the above

6. Identify three things that helped Cameron become a success. Write each answer in a complete sentence.

A. _____

B. _____

C. _____

7. If you started a business, what kind of business would it be? Why? Write a short paragraph on another sheet of paper. Use complete sentences.

Out on the Ice

A girl skated onto the ice. The crowd was silent. She was strong. She moved with the music. She **glided** with feeling. Kristi Yamaguchi was 16 years old. She won two awards that day. No one was surprised.

The next year, Kristi skated at the **World Junior Championships**. She won the gold medal! But, Kristi kept pushing herself. She won 14 other first-place medals. Then, she took a big leap. She skated at the 1992 Winter Olympics.

An American female figure skater had won an Olympic gold medal before. But, that was 16 years ago. Could Kristi be next? She was ready to try. She had been trying all of her life.

Kristi was born with **clubbed feet**. She wore leg casts. Then, she wore special shoes. Walking was hard. Her legs were weak. Kristi's mother wanted her to dance. This would build up Kristi's legs. When Kristi was four years old, she saw the **Olympic Games** on TV. Kristi decided to skate.

Kristi had to practice a lot. She trained six days a week. She got up very early. She skated for five hours. After school, she had skating lessons. Kristi did this for 10 years!

Kristi worked hard. She was ready. Could she win Olympic gold? An older American skater told Kristi to have fun. "Enjoy your skating," he said. "It would show."

So, Kristi had fun. And, it showed! It is hard to skate perfectly. This does not happen many times. For Kristi, the Olympics was one of those times. She won the gold medal! Kristi's hard work paid off.

---

glide: to move smoothly without stopping

World Junior Championships: an international competition held every year for teenaged skaters

clubbed feet: twisted feet that prevent someone from standing with feet flat on the ground

Olympic Games: an international sports festival held every four years

2.RI.4, 2.RI.10, 2.RF.4, 2.L.4

Out on the Ice

A girl skated onto the ice. The crowd was silent. Her skating was powerful. She moved with the music. She **glided** with feeling. Sixteen-year-old Kristi Yamaguchi won two awards that day. No one was surprised.

The next year, Kristi skated at the **World Junior Championships**. She won the gold medal! Kristi kept pushing herself. In four more years, she won 14 other first-place medals. Then, she skated at the 1992 Winter Olympics.

Sixteen years before, an American female figure skater had won Olympic gold. Could Kristi be next? She was ready to try.

Kristi was born with **clubbed feet**. She wore casts on her legs. Later, she wore special shoes. She had trouble walking. Her legs were weak. Kristi's mother wanted her to dance. This would strengthen Kristi's legs. But, when Kristi was four years old, she watched the **Olympic Games** on TV. She told her mother that she wanted to skate.

Kristi practiced a lot, six days a week. She got up at four o'clock in the morning. She skated for five hours. After school, she went to skating lessons. Kristi did this for 10 years!

Kristi worked hard. She was finally trying for an Olympic gold medal. An older American skater told Kristi to have fun. If she enjoyed her skating, it would show.

So, Kristi had fun. And, it showed! Kristi said later that there are not many times when a skater knows that she skated perfectly. For her, the Olympics was one of those times. She won the gold medal. And, she proved that hard work pays off.

---

glide: to move smoothly without stopping
World Junior Championships: an international competition held every year for teenaged skaters
clubbed feet: twisted feet that prevent someone from standing with feet flat on the ground
Olympic Games: an international sports festival held every four years

---

Out on the Ice

The crowd was hushed as the girl skated onto the ice. Her skating was powerful. She moved with the music, **gliding** with feeling. No one was surprised when 16-year-old Kristi Yamaguchi won two awards that day.

The next year, at the **World Junior Championships**, Kristi won the gold medal! Kristi continued pushing herself. In the next four years, she won 14 other first-place medals. Then came the 1992 Winter Olympics.

It had been 16 years since an American female figure skater had won a gold medal. Kristi wanted to be next. She had been trying all of her life.

Kristi was born with **clubbed feet**. She wore heavy casts on her legs. Later, she wore special shoes. She had trouble walking. Kristi's mother wanted her to take dancing lessons to help strengthen Kristi's legs. But, when Kristi was four years old, she watched the **Olympic Games** on TV. She told her mother that she wanted to skate instead.

Six days a week for 10 years, Kristi arose at four o'clock in the morning. She skated for five hours . . . before she started school for the day! After school, she went to skating lessons.

Now, after all of her hard work, Kristi was finally trying for an Olympic gold medal. An older American skater told Kristi to have fun. If she enjoyed her skating, it would show.

Kristi had fun. Kristi said later that there are only a few times in a skater's life when she knows that she skated perfectly. For her, the Olympics was one of those times. She won the gold medal. She proved that hard work pays off.

---

glide: to move smoothly without stopping
World Junior Championships: an international competition held every year for teenaged skaters
clubbed feet: twisted feet that prevent someone from standing with feet flat on the ground
Olympic Games: an international sports festival held every four years

● ● ● ●

Out on the Ice

Answer the questions.

1. Which of the following phrases means the same thing as *pushing herself*?

    A. pulling apart   **B.** working hard
    C. doing push-ups   **D.** falling down

2. Why did Kristi have to have casts on her legs?

    A. She had broken legs.   **B.** She had clapped feet.
    C. She had special shoes.   **D.** She had clubbed feet.

3. Why did Kristi's mother want her to take dance lessons?

    A. to help make her legs strong   **B.** to help make her arms strong
    C. to help her learn how to skate   **D.** A. and C.

Write **T** for true or **F** for false.

4. _____ Kristi won her Olympic gold medal in 1990.

5. _____ Kristi skated for up to three hours before going to school.

6. _____ Kristi's Olympic gold medal was the first one for an American female figure skater in 16 years.

7. How many hours of morning practice did Kristi do in one week?

    A. 5 hours   **B.** 15 hours   **C.** 30 hours   **D.** 50 hours

8. List two adjectives that describe Kristi Yamaguchi's skating.

    A. _____

    B. _____

9. Tell about a time in your life when hard work helped you. Write a short paragraph on another sheet of paper. Use complete sentences. Use the word *myself* at least once in your paragraph.

A Brave Conductor

It was hard for **slaves** to escape from the South. Many slaves tried. Many were caught. In 1849, Harriet Tubman was a slave in Dorchester County, Maryland. She used the Underground Railroad to escape. Harriet followed the North Star. Friendly people let her stay in their houses. She was not caught. Harriet reached Philadelphia, Pennsylvania. Philadelphia was in the North. Slaves were free in the North. Harriet knew that she could live as a free person.

Then, Harriet did something very brave. She did not stay. She went back to the South! She became a **conductor** on the Underground Railroad. She helped other slaves escape. It was a dangerous job.

Harriet found her family. She helped some of them escape to Canada. Over 10 years, Harriet went back many times. She helped about 300 slaves reach freedom.

In 1861, the **American Civil War** began. Harriet spied for the North. She knew the land. She had traveled through it many times in the dark. Harriet could **pose** as a slave. She learned things to help the army in the North.

Soon, African Americans could become soldiers. Harriet helped them too. She even led some soldiers on a bold raid. They freed more than 700 slaves during this raid.

Harriet did not spy all the time. She also was a nurse. She took care of soldiers and slaves. When the war was over, Harriet still worked. She fought for the rights of women and freed slaves. She opened a home in Auburn, New York. Here, she cared for aging African Americans. Harriet died there in 1913.

slave: a person who is owned by someone else
conductor: a person who directs or shows other people how to do something
American Civil War: the US war between the North and the South, 1861–65
pose: to pretend to be someone else

2.RI.4, 2.RI.10, 2.RF.4, 2.L.4

A Brave Conductor

It took courage for **slaves** to try to escape from the South. Many slaves tried. Many were caught. In 1849, Harriet Tubman escaped. She used the Underground Railroad and followed the North Star. She traveled at night, staying with friendly people. She started in Dorchester County, Maryland. She ended in Philadelphia, Pennsylvania. Slaves were free in the North. She knew she could live there as a free person.

Then, Harriet did something very brave. Harriet went back to the South! She worked as a **conductor** on the Underground Railroad. She helped other slaves escape. It was a dangerous job.

First, Harriet found her family. She helped some of them escape to Canada. In the next 10 years, she went back many times. Harriet helped about 300 slaves reach freedom in the North.

In 1861, the **American Civil War** began. What did Harriet do? She became a spy for the North. She knew the land. She had traveled through it many times in the dark. Harriet could **pose** as a slave. She learned information to help the army in the North.

Soon, African Americans could become soldiers. Harriet helped them too. She even led a group of soldiers on a bold raid. Harriet and the soldiers freed more than 700 slaves during the raid.

Harriet did not spy all the time. She also was a nurse. She took care of injured soldiers and slaves. When the war was over, Harriet still worked. She fought for the rights of women and freed slaves. She opened a home in Auburn, New York, where she cared for aging African Americans. Harriet died there in 1913.

slave: a person who is owned by someone else
conductor: a person who directs or shows other people how to do something
American Civil War: the US war between the North and the South, 1861–65
pose: to pretend to be someone else

2.RI.4, 2.RI.10, 2.RF.4, 2.L.4

A Brave Conductor

It took courage for **slaves** to try to escape from the South. Many slaves tried but were caught. In 1849, Harriet Tubman used the Underground Railroad to escape to freedom. The North Star guided her. At night, she stayed with friendly people. She traveled from Dorchester County, Maryland, to Philadelphia, Pennsylvania. She knew that she could live in the North as a free person.

Then, Harriet did something unusual. Instead of staying in the North, Harriet returned to the South! She worked as a **conductor** on the Underground Railroad. She helped other slaves escape. It was a choice filled with danger.

First, Harriet found several of her family members. She helped them escape to Canada. Between 1850 and 1860, she went back many times to help other slaves. Harriet helped as many as 300 slaves reach freedom in the North.

When the **American Civil War** started in 1861, Harriet became a spy for the North. She knew the countryside because she had traveled through it so many times in the dark. Harriet could **pose** as a slave. She learned information to help the army in the North.

When African Americans were allowed to become soldiers, Harriet helped them too. She even led a group of soldiers on a daring raid. Harriet and the soldiers freed more than 700 slaves during the raid.

When she was not on a spy mission, Harriet worked as a nurse. She took care of wounded soldiers and slaves. After the war was over, Harriet fought for the rights of women and freed slaves. She opened a home in Auburn, New York, to care for aging African Americans. She died there in 1913.

slave: a person who is owned by someone else
conductor: a person who directs or shows other people how to do something
American Civil War: the US war between the North and the South, 1861–65
pose: to pretend to be someone else

A Brave Conductor

Answer the questions.

1. The _____ _____ was a pathway that helped slaves escape.

2. When the Civil War started, Harriet worked as a _____ .

3. Before the Civil War, Harriet helped free as many as _____ slaves.

4. Which phrase could best replace *pose as* in the sentence?

   Harriet could pose as a slave.

   A. remain as   **B.** pretend to be   **C.** strike a pose as   **D.** react like

5. Make four new words by combining a root word and a suffix. Circle the new word that is a synonym for the word *brave*.

fear	fully	_____
courage	ly	_____
coward	ous	_____
safe	ty	_____

6. Imagine that you are an escaped slave. Which of the following might keep you from going back to help other slaves?

   A. being caught and put back into slavery
   B. being punished for running away
   C. being put to death for running away
   D. all of the above

7. Can you think of a reason that would make you want to go back to the South if you were an escaped slave? Explain your reason. Write a short paragraph on another sheet of paper. Use complete sentences.

Guiding Star

Sacagawea knew about life in strange places. Her tribe was the **Shoshone**. In 1800, her tribe was raided. Sacagawea was taken far away. She had to live with an enemy tribe. Sacagawea was 12 years old.

Four years later, Sacagawea married a French **trader**. They had a son. That winter, some white men came. They camped nearby. The leaders were Meriwether Lewis and William Clark. President **Thomas Jefferson** had hired them. They were explorers. Lewis and Clark wanted to travel from the Missouri River to the Pacific Ocean.

Lewis and Clark heard of Sacagawea. They were headed west. The Shoshone land was west. Sacagawea had been born there. She knew the land. The men needed horses to cross the mountains. Sacagawea could help. Lewis and Clark hired Sacagawea and her husband.

They left in the spring of 1805. They paddled up the Missouri River. A big storm hit. One boat almost tipped over. Important papers fell into the water. Sacagawea saved them.

Sacagawea was an American Indian woman. Other Indians saw her with the white men. This made them trust the explorers. Sacagawea helped the men talk to different tribes. Sacagawea guided them west.

Lewis and Clark led the group to a Shoshone village. They needed to trade for horses. This village was the home of Sacagawea's brother! The men thought that she would stay. But, Sacagawea did not. She had heard of a "monstrous fish" (a whale). She wanted to see it. Sacagawea stayed with Lewis and Clark. She went all the way to the Pacific Ocean.

Shoshone: an American Indian tribe living in Idaho, Nevada, Wyoming, Montana, Utah, and parts of California

trader: someone who buys and sells things

Thomas Jefferson: the third president of the United States (1801–1809)

Guiding Star

Sacagawea knew about life in strange places. Her tribe, the **Shoshone**, was raided. Sacagawea was taken **captive**. She was 12 years old and was taken hundreds of miles from home. Her home was now with the enemy.

Four years later, Sacagawea married a French **trader**. They had a son. That winter, a group of white men arrived. They camped near the village. The leaders were Meriwether Lewis and William Clark. President **Thomas Jefferson** had hired them to explore the western United States. Lewis and Clark needed to travel from the Missouri River to the Pacific Ocean.

Lewis and Clark heard of Sacagawea. They were headed west toward the Shoshone land. Sacagawea had been born there. She knew the country. The men needed horses to cross the mountains. Sacagawea could help them trade for horses. They hired Sacagawea and her husband.

The group left in the spring of 1805. They paddled up the Missouri River. Soon a big storm hit. One boat almost tipped over. Supplies fell into the water. Sacagawea saved important goods and writings.

Sacagawea was an American Indian woman. Other Indians saw her with the white men. This made them trust the explorers. Sacagawea interpreted their words. She helped the white men talk to different tribes. Sacagawea guided them west.

Lewis and Clark came to a Shoshone village. They needed to trade for horses. This village was the home of Sacagawea's brother! The explorers thought that she would stay. But, Sacagawea chose to go on. She wanted to see a "monstrous fish" (a whale). She traveled all of the way to the Pacific Ocean.

Shoshone: an American Indian tribe living in Idaho, Nevada, Wyoming, Montana, Utah, and parts of California
captive: captured or imprisoned
trader: someone who buys and sells things
Thomas Jefferson: the third president of the United States (1801–1809)

Guiding Star

Sacagawea knew about life in strange places. In 1800, at the age of 12, she was taken **captive**. Her tribe, the **Shoshone**, was raided. Sacagawea was taken hundreds of miles from home to live with an enemy tribe.

Four years later, she married a French **trader** and had a son. That winter, a group of white men camped near the village. The leaders were Meriwether Lewis and William Clark. They were hired by President **Thomas Jefferson** to explore the West from the Missouri River to the Pacific Ocean.

Lewis and Clark learned that Sacagawea had been born in the Shoshone tribe. They were headed west toward the Shoshone land. The explorers needed horses to cross the mountains. Sacagawea could help them trade for horses. Lewis and Clark hired Sacagawea and her husband.

The group left in the spring of 1805. They paddled up the Missouri River into a big storm. One of the boats almost tipped over. Sacagawea saved important goods and writings that had fallen into the water. This was the first of many times that she would help.

Since an American Indian woman was traveling with the group, other Indians trusted the white men. Sacagawea worked as an interpreter. She helped the explorers talk to different tribes. Sacagawea guided the group as they went west toward her childhood home.

Lewis and Clark led their group to a Shoshone village to trade for horses. It was the home of Sacagawea's brother! Lewis and Clark thought that she would stay. But, she wanted to see a "monstrous fish" (a whale). Sacagawea traveled all of the way to the Pacific Ocean with Lewis and Clark's team.

captive: captured or imprisoned
Shoshone: an American Indian tribe living in Idaho, Nevada, Wyoming, Montana, Utah, and parts of California
trader: someone who buys and sells things
Thomas Jefferson: the third president of the United States (1801–1809)

Guiding Star

Answer the questions.

1. Sacagawea was married to a French _____.

2. Sacagawea was born a member of the _____ tribe.

3. A group of explorers led by _____ and _____ camped near Sacagawea's village.

4. The explorers wanted Sacagawea to go with them because

   A. she might remember the land where she had grown up.
   B. they were headed west.
   C. they needed to trade for horses and did not know the language.
   D. all of the above

5. When she left with Lewis and Clark, Sacagawea was

   A. 12 years old.   B. 14 years old.   C. 15 years old.   D. 17 years old.

6. In the first paragraph, the author writes that Sacagawea's tribe was raided. Which word could replace *raided*?

   A. moved   B. befriended   C. attacked   D. built

7. What happened to Sacagawea next after she was taken captive?

   _____

8. Which of the following sentences best summarizes the story?

   A. Sacagawea was a Shoshone woman who had a small baby.
   B. Sacagawea, a Shoshone woman, helped the group of explorers led by Lewis and Clark in many ways.
   C. Lewis and Clark hired Sacagawea and her husband to help them on their journey.
   D. Sacagawea worked as a guide and an interpreter.

9. Would you have agreed to go with Lewis and Clark on their journey? Why or why not? Write a short paragraph on another sheet of paper. Use complete sentences. Make sure you use correct capitalization for any geographic names.

End of the Darkness

In 1882, baby Helen became very sick. She got better. But, something was wrong. She could not see. She could not hear. Helen Keller was blind and deaf.

The next years were awful. Helen was like a wild animal. She screamed. She broke dishes. She threw chairs. Her parents met with **Alexander Graham Bell**. He had invented the telephone. He helped deaf children too. He found a teacher for Helen. Her name was Anne Sullivan. Anne was almost fully blind herself.

Anne calmed Helen. Helen stopped throwing things. She ate neatly. Anne tried to teach Helen. Anne spelled words with her fingers. She would give Helen something to hold. Then, Anne would spell that word into Helen's hand. Helen repeated the movements. But, she did not understand.

In 1887, Anne finally broke through to Helen. Anne pumped water into Helen's hands. Helen felt the wet water. Then, Anne spelled the word water. Helen felt her teacher's fingers. Suddenly, she knew. The movements were words! Water was Helen's first word. She learned 30 words that day!

Anne taught Helen to read. Helen learned **braille**. In braille, raised dots make words. Blind people read the words with their fingertips. Helen was smart. She was the first deaf and blind person to graduate from college!

Anne stayed with Helen. They toured the world. Helen gave talks. Anne translated. In 1903, Helen wrote a book. It was called *The Story of My Life*. Helen received many awards. She was even given the **Presidential Medal of Freedom**. Helen and Anne's story still gives hope to blind and deaf people.

Alexander Graham Bell: a Scottish-born scientist who invented the telephone in 1876

braille: a form of written language for the blind, invented by a blind teacher from France named Louis Braille

Presidential Medal of Freedom: the highest award given to someone during peacetime

End of the Darkness

In 1882, baby Helen became very sick. When she got better, something was still wrong. She could not see. She could not hear. Helen Keller was blind and deaf.

Helen was like a wild animal. She screamed. She broke dishes. She threw chairs. Her parents wanted to help her. They met with **Alexander Graham Bell**. He had invented the telephone, but he also worked with deaf children. Mr. Bell found a teacher for Helen. Her name was Anne Sullivan. Anne was almost fully blind herself.

Anne helped Helen to calm down. She learned to sit at a table. She ate neatly. She stopped throwing things. Anne tried to teach Helen how to spell words with her fingers. She would give Helen something, like a doll. Then, she would spell the word in Helen's hand. But, Helen did not understand.

In 1887, Anne finally broke through to Helen's lonely world. The teacher pumped water into Helen's hands. Then, she spelled the word water. Suddenly, Helen understood that Anne's movements were words. The words told her about the world. Helen learned 30 words that very day!

Anne taught Helen how to read **braille**. Braille is a system of raised dots. The dots make words. Blind people read these with their fingertips. Helen was the first deaf and blind person to graduate from college.

Anne stayed with Helen for the rest of her life. They toured the world together. In 1903, Helen wrote *The Story of My Life*. Helen received many awards. She was given the **Presidential Medal of Freedom**. Helen Keller and Anne Sullivan's story still gives hope to blind and deaf people today.

Alexander Graham Bell: a Scottish-born scientist who invented the telephone in 1876

braille: a form of written language for the blind, invented by a blind teacher from France named Louis Braille

Presidential Medal of Freedom: the highest award given to someone during peacetime

End of the Darkness

In 1880, baby Helen became very sick. She recovered. But, she did not **respond** to voices or lights. Helen Keller, not yet two, had become blind and deaf.

The next years were terrible. Helen would scream, break dishes, and flip chairs. Her parents met with **Alexander Graham Bell**, inventor of the telephone. He also worked with deaf children. Bell helped find a teacher for Helen. The teacher's name was Anne Sullivan. Anne was almost completely blind herself.

With Anne's help, Helen calmed down. She learned to sit at a table, eat her food, and stop throwing things. Anne tried to teach Helen how to spell words with her fingers. She would give Helen an item, like a doll, and spell the word in Helen's hand. But Helen did not understand what they meant.

In 1887, Anne finally broke through to Helen's dark, lonely world. Anne pumped water into Helen's hands and spelled the word *water*. Suddenly, Helen understood that the finger movements were words.

Anne taught Helen how to read **braille**. Braille is a system of raised dots that can be read with the fingertips. Helen was very smart. She became the first deaf and blind person to earn a college degree.

Anne stayed with Helen for the rest of her life. In 1903, Helen wrote *The Story of My Life*. Helen received many awards, including the **Presidential Medal of Freedom**. Their story continues to give hope to blind and deaf people everywhere. They are an inspiration.

---

respond: to react to someone or something
Alexander Graham Bell: a Scottish-born scientist who invented the telephone in 1876
braille: a form of written language for the blind, invented by a blind teacher from France named Louis Braille
Presidential Medal of Freedom: the highest award given to someone during peacetime

End of the Darkness

Answer the questions.

Write **T** for true or **F** for false.

1. _____ Helen Keller learned to read when she was five years old.

2. _____ Helen Keller graduated from college.

3. Circle the correct word or phrase in parentheses to complete each of the following sentences.

   A. Before Anne Sullivan became her teacher, Helen (wept, cried, screamed) a lot.

   B. On the day that Helen finally understood her teacher's spelling movements, Helen felt a (drop, dribble, flow) of water gush over her hand.

   C. Anne Sullivan could see (almost nothing, well, normally)

4. Which of the following is an opinion?

   A. Anne Sullivan would give Helen an object and then spell its name in her hand.

   B. To be both blind and deaf must be scary.

   C. Anne and Helen toured the world together.

   D. Anne Sullivan stayed with Helen Keller for the rest of her life.

5. What is *braille*?

   A. It is a code of raised dots that blind people read with their fingertips.

   B. It is a way of spelling with fingers in order to help blind people learn words.

   C. It is a method of using high and low sounds for people who cannot hear most sounds.

   D. It is a series of colorful letters that help people learn to read.

6. Which do you think would be harder to lose: your sight or your hearing? Why do you think so? Write a short paragraph on another sheet of paper. Use complete sentences.

As Dry as a Bone

One of Earth's driest places is in Chile. It is the Atacama Desert. No rain has fallen on parts of the desert in 400 years! The desert is not very wet anywhere. It gets less than one-third of an inch (0.85 cm) of water every year. Most of this is from fog.

The Atacama Desert is close to water. The Amazon River is on one side. The Pacific Ocean is on the other side. Why is the desert so dry? The Andes Mountains are in the way. They hold the rain over the Amazon rain forest. The rain cannot reach the desert.

The Atacama is not hot. That is because it is high. It is almost 8,000 feet (2,438.4 m) above sea level. Temperatures go down to 32°F (0°C). A hot day is only about 77°F (25°C).

The Atacama is a harsh place. But, there is life. A few plants grow here. They have long roots. The roots must reach water deep in the ground. Insects live here too. They eat the plants. So do foxes and **llamas**.

The Atacama has salt lakes. They were made during the last **ice age**. Red algae grow in the lakes. **Flamingos** fly across the Atacama. They stop at the salt lakes. They do not drink the water. But, they eat the red algae. This makes their feathers pink!

Humans also live here. Some live in villages in the desert. Many live in towns by the coast. Tourists visit these towns. And, how do tourists stay dry? They visit the desert!

llama: a large, woolly pack animal related to the camel
ice age: a period of time long ago when sheets of ice, or glaciers, covered much of the earth
flamingo: a tall, pink wading bird with long legs and neck

As Dry as a Bone

Do you want to be dry? Go to the Atacama Desert! It is in Chile. It has not rained in parts of the desert for 400 years! It is not very wet anywhere in the desert. It rarely rains. The desert gets less than one-third of an inch (0.85 cm) of water every year. Most of this comes from fog. The Atacama is one of the driest places on Earth.

The Amazon River is on one side of the desert. The Pacific Ocean is on the other side. Why is the desert so dry? The Andes Mountains are in the way! The mountains hold the rain over the Amazon rain forest. The rain cannot reach the desert.

The Atacama is not a hot desert. It is cool. That is because it is high. The average height above sea level is almost 8,000 feet (2,438.4 m). Temperatures range from 32°F (0°C) to 77°F (25°C).

The Atacama is a harsh place. But, there is life. Plants and animals always find a way to survive. Even in the desert. A few plants grow here. They have long roots. The roots have to reach water deep in the ground. Insects and some animals, like foxes and **llamas**, eat the plants.

There are salt lakes in the desert. They were made during the last **ice age**. **Flamingos** fly to the salty lakes. They do not drink the water. Instead, they eat a type of red algae that grows there. This food is what makes their feathers pink.

Humans also live here. They live in tiny villages across the desert. They live in large towns along the ocean coast. Tourists visit these towns. And, sometimes they visit the Atacama Desert too.

llama: a large, woolly pack animal related to the camel

ice age: a period of time long ago when sheets of ice, or glaciers, covered much of the earth

flamingo: a tall, pink wading bird with long legs and neck

As Dry as a Bone

Take a trip to the Atacama Desert in Chile. In some parts of the desert, it has not rained for 400 years! In other parts, less than one-third of an inch (0.85 cm) of water falls every year. Most of that comes from fog. This is one of the driest places on Earth.

Why is the Atacama Desert so dry? It lies between the wet Amazon River and the even wetter Pacific Ocean. But, the Andes Mountains are in the way. They trap rain and hold it over the Amazon rain forest. The desert, on the opposite side of the mountains, gets none. The Atacama is a cool desert. The average elevation, or height above sea level, is almost 8,000 feet (2,438.4 m). The temperature ranges from 32°F (0°C) to 77°F (25°C).

However, there is life here. In all harsh places on Earth, some plants and animals have discovered ways to survive. A few plants grow in the Atacama. These plants have long roots that reach water deep in the ground. Insects and a few animals, such as foxes and **llamas**, eat these plants.

Salt lakes in the desert were made with water from the last **ice age**. Big flocks of **flamingos** fly to the salty lakes. They do not drink the water. Instead, they eat a type of red algae that grows there. Their **diet** is what makes their feathers so pink.

Another animal has found a way to live in the Atacama: human beings. They live in tiny villages scattered across the desert. They also live in large towns built along the coast of the Pacific Ocean. Many tourists arrive in these towns and take day trips into the huge, dry desert all around them.

---

llama: a large, woolly pack animal related to the camel
ice age: a period of time long ago when sheets of ice, or glaciers, covered much of the earth
flamingo: a tall, pink wading bird with long legs and neck
diet: the kind of food that an animal usually eats

2.RI.1, 2.RI.6, 2.W.1, 2.L.3, 2.L.4

As Dry as a Bone

Answer the questions.

1. Which of the following is the best description of the Atacama Desert?

    A. It is a very large desert with mountains on one side.
    B. It is one of the driest places on Earth.
    C. It is one of the driest places on Earth, and it is a desert in Chile near the Andes Mountains.
    D. It is very dry, but some animals still live there, including human beings.

2. The author uses the word *harsh* to describe places such as the Atacama Desert. What is a synonym for *harsh*?

    A. healthy   **B.** safe   **C.** useless   **D.** severe

3. The _____ Mountains trap rain.

4. They hold the rain over the Amazon _____ _____.

5. The Atacama Desert receives _____ rain as a result.

6. Which of the following is an opinion?

    A. Flamingos eat algae from the salt lakes in the Atacama Desert.
    B. The Atacama Desert must be the hardest place on Earth to live.
    C. The Atacama Desert has some villages and towns.
    D. Some animals cannot live in the Atacama Desert.

7. It does not rain very much in the Atacama Desert. The desert gets most of its water from _____.

8. What do you think the author's main purpose was in writing this story? Write your answer in one or two complete sentences.

    _____

    _____

    _____

9. Would you like to go to the Atacama Desert? Why or why not? Write a short paragraph on another sheet of paper. Use complete sentences.

The Amazing Amazon

Water runs from rivers to seas. River water is fresh. Seawater is salty. One-fifth of this freshwater comes from just one river. Which one? The huge Amazon River! The Amazon is in South America. It is near the rain forest.

The Amazon River starts in the mountains. It runs over 4,000 miles (6,437.38 km). It **flows** into the Atlantic Ocean. A river mouth is where a river meets the sea. River water runs into the sea. The Amazon holds a lot of water. Its mouth is 150 miles (241.4 km) wide!

Explorers found the river mouth in 1500. They were on the Atlantic Ocean. They were 200 miles (321.87 km) from land. All they could see was water. But, it was not salt water. They were sailing on freshwater! How could that be? The water was from the Amazon River.

The Amazon River has not changed much. People cut down rain forest trees. They cut down a lot of trees! But, not many humans live here. The Amazon River does not have any bridges. Is this why there are so many strange living things?

Catfish live in the Amazon. They grow very large. One catfish can weigh 200 pounds (90.72 kg). That is as big as a man! A dolphin swims in the Amazon. It is the boto, or pink river dolphin. It lives in freshwater.

Scary creatures live here too. One is the piranha. The piranha is a fish. But, be careful! This fish has sharp teeth. It eats meat! An **anaconda** is a snake. It is one of the world's biggest snakes. The anaconda floats under the water. It is hard to see. Only its nose and eyes peek out.

The Amazon River is full of life. The rain forest is full of life too. Thousands of animals live here. The Amazon River is amazing!

flow: move smoothly and continuously
catfish: a fish with sharp whiskers around its mouth
anaconda: a huge snake related to the boa

The Amazing Amazon

Water runs from rivers into seas. River water is fresh. Seawater is salty. About one-fifth of this freshwater comes from one river called the Amazon River. This river is in South America, near the Amazon rain forest.

The Amazon River starts high up in the **Andes Mountains**. It winds over 4,000 miles (6,437.38 km). Water **flows** from the Amazon River into the Atlantic Ocean. A river mouth is where a river meets the sea. River water dumps into the sea. The Amazon River carries a lot of water. Its mouth has to be huge. The Amazon river mouth is 150 miles (241.4 km) wide!

Explorers discovered the river mouth in 1500, while sailing on the Atlantic Ocean. They were 200 miles (321.87 km) from land. But, they were not sailing on salt water. They were sailing on fresh water from the mouth of the Amazon River!

The Amazon River has not changed much since then. People cut down a lot of rain forest trees. Few humans live there. There are no bridges built across the Amazon. Maybe this is why there are so many strange creatures.

Catfish live in the Amazon and grow very large. One catfish can weigh 200 pounds (90.72 kg)! A dolphin swims in the Amazon. It is the boto, or pink river dolphin. It can live in freshwater.

Scary creatures live in the Amazon too. One is the piranha. This fish has sharp teeth. And, it eats meat! An **anaconda** is an enormous snake. It floats just under the water. Only its nose and eyes peek out.

Thousands of other animals live nearby. They live in the Amazon rain forest. They all help make the Amazon River amazing!

Andes Mountains: the biggest mountain range in South America
flow: move smoothly and continuously
catfish: a fish with sharp whiskers around its mouth
anaconda: a huge snake related to the boa

The Amazing Amazon

South America's Amazon River is a mighty force. About one-fifth of all freshwater that enters Earth's oceans comes from this single river.

The Amazon River winds down from the **Andes Mountains**. It flows over 4,000 miles (6,437.38 km) to reach the sea. The mouth of a river is where the river meets the ocean. The mouth of the Amazon River is enormous, measuring over 150 miles (241.4 km) wide.

Explorers discovered the mouth of the Amazon River in 1500. Their ship on the Atlantic Ocean was 200 miles (321.87 km) from land. They were surrounded by water. But, the sailors found that they were sailing on freshwater, not salt water! This water came from the huge mouth of the Amazon River.

The Amazon has not been changed much by humans over the years. Few people live in the surrounding rain forest. Rain forest trees are being cut down at a fast rate. But, the Amazon River does not have a single bridge built across it. Maybe the shortage of people is the reason why the Amazon is home to so many **unique** fish and animals.

Catfish in the Amazon can weigh up to 200 pounds (90.72 kg). A type of freshwater river dolphin, called a boto, or pink river dolphin, lives here. A meat-eating fish called the piranha also swims in the river. These scary fish have extremely sharp teeth. One of the largest snakes in the world is the **anaconda**. It lives in the Amazon River too. The anaconda floats just under the surface of the water, with only its nose and eyes visible.

These animals share the Amazon River with thousands of rare animals in the nearby rain forest. They all help make the Amazon River truly amazing!

Andes Mountains: the biggest mountain range in South America
unique: not like anything else
catfish: a fish with sharp whiskers around its mouth
anaconda: a huge snake related to the boa

The Amazing Amazon

Answer the questions.

1. The mouth of the Amazon River is very wide. Which word could replace *mouth* in this sentence?

    A. lips   **B.** opening   **C.** flow   **D.** water

2. The Amazon River is

    A. the longest river in North America.
    B. a supplier of one-fifth of the world's freshwater.
    C. a river that starts in the Rocky Mountains.
    D. a river surrounded by plains.

3. According to the story, what clue helped explorers know that a huge river was nearby?

    A. They were sailing on the sea, but the water under their ship was freshwater.
    B. They heard the roar of the river pouring into the sea.
    C. They saw types of fish that usually live in rivers.
    D. all of the above

4. Which of the following does not live in the Amazon River?

    A. catfish   **B.** anaconda   **C.** blue whale   **D.** piranha

5. The story describes all of the following except

    A. what piranhas eat.
    B. why botos are also called pink river dolphins.
    C. what anacondas look like in the water.
    D. how much the Amazon catfish can grow to weigh.

6. Would you want to go sailing on the Amazon River? Why or why not? Write a short paragraph on another sheet of paper. Use complete sentences. Use a dictionary to check the spelling of any strange animals that you might meet on the Amazon.

Answer Key

Page 7

1. D; 2. C; 3. B; 4. Answers will vary but must include explanation from story, such as sharp little hairs, and be written in a complete sentence. 5. Answers will vary but must include three appropriate adjectives from story. 6. friendly, loud, big-billed, meat-eating; 7. Answers will vary but must present opinion and reasons and ways in which the texts are similar and different.

Page 11

1. D; 2. A; 3. E; 4. B; 5. C; 6. C; 7. Answers must finish a complete sentence. A. because it needs to save energy, B. upside down, C. snakes, birds; 8. A. does not, B. 20, C. night, D. claws; 9. Answers will vary but should include reasons from the text such as food and safety. 10. Answers will vary but must present an opinion and reasons.

Page 15

1. B; 2. C; 3. B; 4. Answers will vary but may include the opinion that dolphins communicate in a special language; answer must be written in one or two complete sentences. 5. D; 6. F; 7. T; 8. F; 9. F; 10. Answers will vary but must present appropriate text from the story.

Page 19

1. C; 2. D; 3. B; 4. C; 5. A; 6. A; 7. A; 8. Answers will vary but must present an opinion and reasons.

Page 23

1. C; 2. D; 3. A; 4. B; 5. D; 6. B; 7. missing link; 8. Answers will vary but must include thinker Zhu Xi and scientist Don Gebo. 9. C; 10. Answers will vary but must present an opinion and reasons and ways in which the texts are similar and different.

Page 27

1. B; 2. D; 3. D; 4. C; 5. A; 6. C; 7. B; 8. Answers will vary but must include correct capitalization. 9. Answers will vary but must present an opinion and reasons.

Page 31

1. B; 2. C; 3. B; 4. B; 5. Answers will vary but must include wooden and steel and be written in a complete sentence. 6. A; 7. Answers will vary but must present an opinion and reasons and include a proper letter greeting and closing.

Page 35

1. D; 2. E; 3. A; 4. B; 5. C; 6. Answers will vary but may include childhood, everyone, himself, oneself, roadtrip, songwriter. 7. A. do, B. was not, C. 35; 8. D; 9. Answers will vary but must present reasons.

Page 39

1. C; 2. C; 3. A; 4. D; 5. A; 6. Answers will vary but must include details from the story and be written in complete sentences. 7. Answers will vary but must present an opinion and reasons.

Page 43

1. B; 2. D; 3. A; 4. F; 5. F; 6. T; 7. C; 8. Answers will vary but may include strong, powerful, award-winning, perfect, or gliding. 9. Answers will vary but must present an opinion and reasons, and use the word *myself*.

Page 47

1. Underground Railroad; 2. spy; 3. 300; 4. B; 5. fearfully, courageous (circled), cowardly, safety or safely; 6. D; 7. Answers will vary but must present an opinion and reasons.

Page 51

1. trader; 2. Shoshone; 3. Lewis, Clark; 4. D; 5. D; 6. C; 7. She was taken hundreds of miles from her home. 8. B; 9. Answers will vary but must present an opinion and reasons.

Page 55

1. F; 2. T; 3. A. screamed, B. flow, C. almost nothing; 4. B; 5. A; 6. Answers will vary but must present an opinion and reasons.

Page 59

1. C; 2. D; 3. Andes; 4. rain forest; 5. Answers may include *little* or *no*. 6. B; 7. fog; 8. Answers will vary but must include details from the story. 9. Answers will vary but must present an opinion and reasons.

Page 63

1. B; 2. B; 3. A; 4. C; 5. B; 6. Answers will vary but must present an opinion and reasons and correct spelling.

Notes

_____

_____

_____

_____